CAERNARFON

In Days Gone By

Katie Withersby Lench

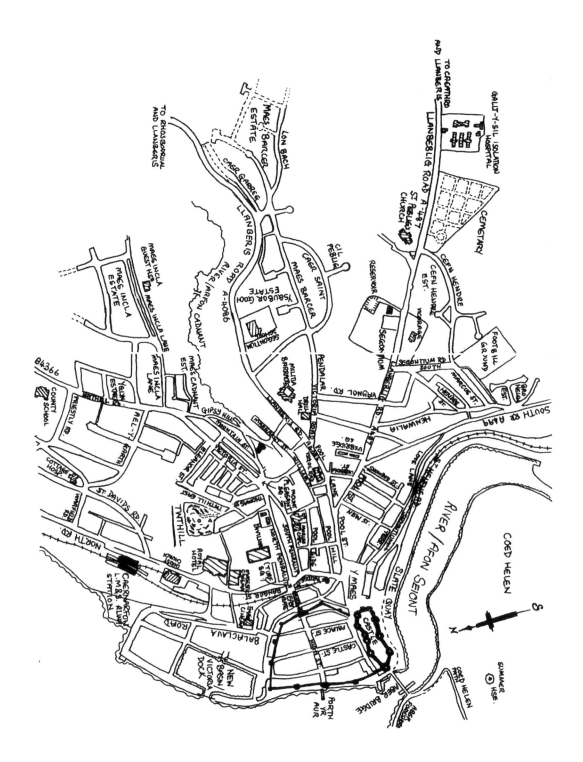

CAERNARFON
In Days Gone By

Katie Withersby Lench

Guidelines Booksales

For all Cofis at home and abroad
&
In memory of those in these photos who are no longer with us.

Published in the UK by:
Guideslines Book Sales
11 Belmont Road
Ipstones
Stoke on Trent
Staffordshire
ST10 2JN
Email: author.porter@gmail.com
Tel: 07971 990649

1st Edition

ISBN 978-184306-505-0

Katie Withersby Lench 2012

Printed by: 4 Edge Ltd, 7A Eldon Way, Hockley, Essex SS5 4AD
Design: Jenksdesign@yahoo.co.uk

Contents

INTRODUCTION

The Castle is sited at the heart of Caernarfon and is truly its most iconic image, but like any town its true heart and spirit is the people who live, visit, work, shop and play there. When asked to define the spirit of Caernarfon of yesteryear, the overwhelming opinion of today's townsfolk (the Cofis as they call themselves) was the strength of community spirit; the people who had little but shared what they had and helped each other as the could in times of hardship. Everybody knew each other and, as it seems to me, everybody still does. The spirit of Caernarfon persists.

The pages of this book will walk you through Caernarfon's historic streets in the company of the men and women who stood behind the camera lens and captured the moments in time which transport us back into their world; the events, buildings and places they considered important or momentous, scenes from daily life, changes to the town and the goings-on of the town's citizens and visitors through a century of photographic images.

There are many stories to be read in these pictures from Caernarfon's past and we can only discern the most obvious and bring back memories of Caernarfon as it looked in the decades of the nineteenth and twentieth centuries. For me this book is not just a quick flick through still images of a distant time, but each one a 'stage set' in which we can pick out individuals, whether we know them or not, and try to imagine how their lives fitted into the surroundings we see them in.

Whatever is important to you about these photographs, they are a treasure trove of information about the town you live in or visit. I hope you enjoy them as much as I do.

Saif y Castell yn ganolbwynt i Gaernarfon ac yn wir, dyma'i delwedd fwyaf eiconig, ond fel unrhyw dref, ei gwir galon a'i hysbryd yw'r bobl sy'n byw, yn ymweld, yn gweithio, yn siopa ac yn chwarae yma.

O ofyn iddynt ddiffinio ysbryd y Gaernarfon a fu, barn unfrydol pobl y dref heddiw (y Cofis fel y'u gelwir) oedd cryfder yr ysbryd cymunedol; y bobl nad oedd ganddynt lawer ond a rannai'r hyn oedd ganddynt gan helpu'i gilydd, fel y gallent, mewn cyfnodau o galedi. Roedd pawb yn adnabod ei gilydd ac, o'r hyn a welaf i, mae pawb yn dal i wneud hynny. Mae ysbryd Caernarfon yn parhau.

Bydd tudalennau'r llyfr hwn yn mynd â chi drwy strydoedd hanesyddol Caernarfon yng nghwmni'r dynion a'r menywod a safodd y tu ôl i lens y camera gan ddal y munudau mewn amser sy'n mynd â ni nôl i'w byd hwy; y digwyddiadau, yr adeiladau a'r llefydd yr oeddent hwy'n eu hystyried yn bwysig neu'n gofiadwy, golygfeydd o fywyd bob dydd, newidiadau i'r drefn a hanesion am ddinasyddion ac ymwelwyr y dref drwy ganrif o ddelweddau ffotograffig.

Mae yna lawer o storïau i'w darllen yn y lluniau hyn o orffennol Caernarfon, a gallwn ni ond dirnad y mwyaf amlwg er mwyn adfer atgofion o Gaernarfon fel yr edrychai yn negawdau'r bedwaredd ganrif ar bymtheg a'r ugeinfed. I mi, nid cip sydyn drwy ddelweddau llonydd amser pell yn ôl yw'r llyfr hwn, ond mae pob un yn 'set llwyfan' lle gallwn ni weld unigolion - efallai y byddwn yn eu hadnabod, efallai ddim ond gallwn geisio dychmygu'r modd yr oedd eu bywydau'n toddi i'r amgylchoedd o'u cwmpas.

Beth bynnag sy'n bwysig i chi yn y lluniau hyn, maent yn drysor o wybodaeth am y dref yr ydych yn byw ynddi neu'n ymweld â hi. Gobeithio y gwnewch eu mwynhau gymaint â mi.

NORMAN WILKINSON. R.I.

LMS

Dominated by its mighty castle, Caernarvon lies to-day in peaceful seclusion facing the quiet waters of the Menai Strait. But it has a history as stirring as that of any fortified place in our land. The first Edward built it and held it for many years against the Welsh, foremost amongst them, Owen Glendower and his hosts: and it played its part again in the Parliamentary Wars of the Seventeenth Century. The Castle is in an excellent state of preservation, and is one of the most glorious monuments to Feudalism in the Country.

CAERNARVON CASTLE

The London, Midland and Scottish Railway issued this poster to attract holidaymakers to Caernarfon
(Science and Society Picture Library)

Caernarfon Castle from the River Seiont

TOURIST TOWN

Tourists have been visiting Caernarfon since the eighteen hundreds when intrepid explorers found Europe closed to them by continental wars. Gathering their nerve they negotiated the hazardous route around Penmaenmawr by horse and carriage and thence into the heart of Snowdonia. Caernarfon was a significant town where accommodation and entertainment might be found. These people were largely the well off who could afford to make these journeys; the people whose work or status did not require them to stay put in their native part of the UK.

The nineteenth century saw the rise of the holidaymaker when many workers used their annual week's unpaid leave to travel out of the towns and cities to the seaside or the country. What made this possible was the speeding force of the train, which made its snaking way along the North Wales coast, arriving in Caernarfon in the 1850s. The town was not slow to respond to the tourist influx and by 1868 the number of hotels advertising in the local trade directory had increased to six, including three on Bangor Street, on the way into the town from the station, one on Castle Street and two on Castle Square (y Maes) itself.

Castle Square (known as 'y Maes' in Welsh) in Caernarfon circa 1900.
The Britannia Inn is at the far left hand lower corner, at an angle to the square

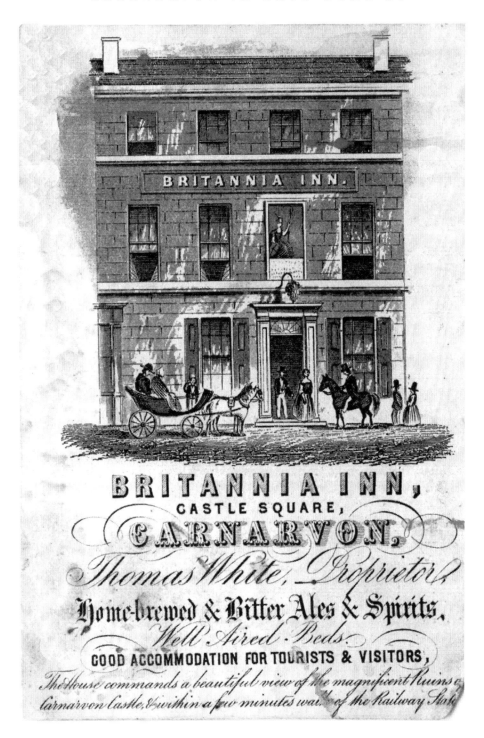

In this 1868 advert for the Britannia Inn on Castle Square the reassuring message assures
'GOOD ACCOMMODATION FOR TOURISTS AND VISITORS'

The Royal Hotel (Bangor Street) and Royal & Sportsman Hotel (Castle Street) also advertised themselves in the trade directory for the same year as specifically suitable for families. Additionally, in the same year thirteen houses in the town advertised themselves as taking in lodgers, and there would be other boarding houses who could not afford to advertise in the trade directories, but simply posted a card in their front windows advertising rooms for holidaymakers.

Crowds of travellers at Caernarfon Station c. 1928

The twentieth century saw the tourist trade rise as people's standards of living improved and trade unions negotiated paid annual leave in the various industries. The North Wales coast became a popular tourist destination for the holidaymakers from Liverpool, Manchester and the Midlands. By the time this photograph was taken, visitors had yet more places to choose from for their lodgings.

*The Eagles Hotel hoped to attract both commercial travellers and tourists with this advert
in the Gateway to Snowdonia Handbook in 1933*

North Road itself would have been a genteel view to greet the weary tourist fresh from a train journey. The row of villas gives way at the back of the photograph to a selection of detached houses each one designed by a local architect in the middle of the nineteenth century. Their views, once of the Strait over the railway station are now of the Strait over Morrison's carpark and filling station. The sunsets are still as glorious as ever, but the calm, traffic free scenes in this picture are long gone! Most visitors would be destined for the centre of the town, whether they were checking into a hotel or boarding house and Bangor Street took them into the heart of Caernarfon.

North Road villas opposite the Railway Station

Bangor Street, Carnarvon

Bangor Street (early 20th century), taken from Turf Square looking out of town

The Ship and Castle pub on the left and what is today the Carlton Bakery on the right. The first building (partially seen) on the right was Caernarfon's Institute and first Free Library.

Williams Jones & Son

WATCH AND CLOCK MAKERS
Jewellers, Engravers, Silversmiths & Opticians

22 BANGOR ST., CARNARVON

A varied stock of Novelties suitable for Wedding and Birthday Gifts.
——— Magnificent stock of DIAMOND and other GEM RINGS. ———
THE WELSH HERALDIC ROYAL SOUVENIR SPOON as
presented to Her Majesty the Queen and H.R.H. the Prince of Wales.
REPAIRS OF EVERY DESCRIPTION.   WEDDING RINGS.
——— Agents for Royal Worcester, Doulton and Goss China ———

W. William Jones & Son, watch and clockmakers

A stalwart of Bangor Street from the 1880s, William Jones at No. 22 sold jewellery and advertised himself as optician, in addition to the watch and clock-making for which the establishment was well known for over sixty years. Optometry and the dispensing of spectacles were not regulated professions until 1958 and old photographs of jewellers and chemists regularly display advertisements offering the services of an optician.

From the *Carnarvon & Denbigh Herald*, December 17th. 1909:

"Before making their Xmas purchases, our readers will do well to glance down this column, and see what the best known establishments in the town have on sale, and what are the chief attractions in the windows ... Mr. W. Williams Jones, Bangor Street, has an excellent display at his magnificent establishment. The windows are very tastefully set out with an assortment of gold and silver watches, gold bangles, and choice silver goods suitable for presents. The Goss china which Mr. Jones exhibits in his establishment is especially worthy of notice. Mr. Jones also furnishes eye glasses and spectacles at most reasonable prices, and his establishment is undoubtedly one of the most up-to-date in North Wales."

Turf Square 1905, from Bangor Street, looking down towards Eastgate Street

The Williams and Pierce general drapery shop 'Y Afr Aur' (Golden Goat) is the shop facing the photographer at the right of the picture. At the back of the photograph you can see the Porth Mawr (Great Gate) of the town walls with the Guildhall astride it.

An Edwardian view of Castle Square / Y Maes

At the end of their walk from the station the traveller finally emerged into the centre of town – Castle Square, which local people call simply 'y Maes'. (Maes meaning an area such as a field or as in this case, a square.) A Maes is a place where things happen and things certainly happen here on the Maes in Caernarfon.

Castle Square / Y Maes circa 1930 (12)

Whether a visitor arrived in the Maes in the nineteenth, twentieth or even twenty first century there are four consistent things that could and still can be found

The first is perhaps the most obvious – the Castle itself, dominating the town as permanent as a landscape feature, a fixture linking the town to its very origins and founder Edward I. To the uninitiated it holds the eye as it was meant to, and to the regular visitor it is a feature looked for as a point of journey's end, perhaps as they clambered down from one of these buses.

Perhaps due to the influx of tourists, two hundred years of neglect to the Castle structure was halted in the 1870s with a programme of works to repair steps, battlements and roofs. Meanwhile the interior of the Castle had been used for many purposes including the keeping of animals. An open space in the centre of a town is never wasted!

Once the eye had been satisfied with the view of the Castle, thoughts must surely have turned to refreshment. Meeting the needs of hungry and thirsty visitors has surely been big business on y Maes for as long as they have been arriving. In addition to the hostelries, notably the Castle Hotel, the Britannia Hotel and the Morgan Lloyd, numerous cafes and tea rooms have come and gone over the years.

The Castle Hotel has a long history of offering refreshment and rooms to visitors to the town, which continues today

The white painted building at the centre of the picture advertises Refreshment Rooms

At the turn of the twentieth century the tourist looking for lunch could try the Refreshment Rooms at the Pool Street end of the Maes. If you look carefully at this photo, a waitress stands on the balcony of the first floor perhaps washing the windows in anticipation of the event that has brought Caernarfon out en-masse, or more likely, using washing the windows as an excuse to get a better view!

The People's Café was a well
known meeting place in the mid
20th century and if the day was
sunny and the visitor wanted to
enjoy the fresh air, they could
always pop along to Bertorelli's
sweet shop where Signor
Bertorelli with his impressive
moustache would sell them his
home made ice cream.

The People's Café (above)
Signor Bertorelli (right)

Market Day in Castle Square / Y Maes, 1987

Having secured their lodgings, satisfied their thirst or hunger and viewed the castle, the fourth thing that visitor throughout the years could and still can do is visit the market. Caernarfon is fortunate that the Maes has retained many of its key buildings over the years. In 1987 the market filled the pedestrianised section and while Morgan Lloyd remains to offer refreshment, the People's Café had become the Cadora Café.

Like any good tourist town, the local bus companies ran tours to key tourist destinations like Llanberis, Bala and Harlech. For as long as coaches both horsedrawn and motorised had run to Caernarfon their destination was the Maes where passengers boarded and alighted.

By the 1930s the Chester-based Crosville Motor Services had services all over north Wales and a booking office here in Caernarfon on the Maes next door to Signor Bertorelli's shop

Whiteways of Waunfawr Coach Booking Office in Caernarfon

Whiteways had been running local services and coach trips in the area since the 1920s.

The picturesque local village of Beddgelert was (and remains!) a popular destination for coach trips

In 1933 a two shilling return excursion ticket on a Crosville motor coach would take you from the Maes to the village of Beddgelert perhaps for afternoon tea if you could afford it. Or, if you had 2/8 to spare you could take a trip to visit Criccieth for a day on the beach, or to visit the castle.

Crosville were still running services in the Caernarfon area in the 1960s

The driver of this bus eats his lunch on the top deck of his bus, parked up at the Crosville Depot on North Street (now demolished and replaced by Asda super-market)

In 1965 Crosville introduced the Cymru Coastliner which anti-cipated the closure of the railway and brought visitors in from Chester and along the coast.
Despite Crosville's deter-mination during the mid twentieth century to buy out the local 'one-man-band' companies in the villages (running often on decommissioned World War One vehicles) there was (and still is) still a choice of bus services serving Caernarfon, and visitors could take tours from Caernarfon with old local companies such as Whiteways and Silver Star, amongst others. In 2010 Silver Star now has its own coach booking office in the old Crosville office on the Maes, but Crosville is no more.

A Silver Star bus waiting on the Maes for passengers in the mid 1970s.

Behind it you can see the neo-Gothic arches of the Caernarfon Herald office which was later burnt down.

Pool Street before pedestrianisation

The Clynnog and Trefor Bus Company retained its independence for many years, serving the coastline south of Caernarfon. One of their buses can be seen here on Pool Street before pedestrianisation, just passing Roberts & Owen Jewellers.

Not only has Silver Star outlived many of its rival tour companies, but back in 1979 the mural artist Edward Povey made Silver Star and its owner one of the focal points of his Caernarfon mural entitled 'Helter Skelter'. The mural was one of the first things visitors would see as they arrived by bus or even, by then, by car. Unfortunately it is now partly covered over by the library building, but still worth a good look to see all the elements of Caernarfon's history which the artist has incorporated into the image. The image was commissioned as part of the National Eisteddfod celebrations when it took place in Caernarfon in 1979 (see overleaf).

The Silver Star bus and owner (seen leaning against the front of the bus) were immortalised in Edward Povey's Caernarfon mural

HOME TOWN

CAERNARVON.

Wigstead's view of Caernarfon in 1799 clearly showing the future Maes as a mound.
(National Library of Wales photo)

A little bit of history... The area known as the Maes was once part of the enclosed area (bailey) of Caernarfon's eleventh century Norman castle and after the Welsh regained the town in the twelfth century it was a garden in the Welsh court on the same site (Llys). After Edward I established his town here, the Maes is generally believed to have been the site of a medieval market place. [1] Today it's handily flat, easy to walk across or drive around, but this wasn't always so. Until 1817, as you can see from this drawing, there was a distinct mound in front of the Castle on the Queen Eleanor's Gate side. Flat land is of course at a premium in an expanding town and in 1817 Caernarfon Corporation paid the unemployed poor to move the earth down to the Quay as part of the extensions to that vital riverside facility, and thus created a better view for the houses which were newly built on the north east side of the square. The Maes had started its transformation from rough ground to handsome town square.

Llanbeblig Choir ready and waiting to set off on an outing in a motor carriage (charabanc).
September 1921

The Maes always used to be the place where over the years the long distance carriages, the motor coaches and then the buses stopped; buses to the local villages and places far away, tourist coaches and charabancs taking Cofis on outings too. This meant that the square was always busy with people arriving, departing and waiting for their bus home from work, shopping, a night out or a day away until 10pm when the last buses to the outlying villages departed. On dark evenings the Maes was lit by the oil lamps of the market traders – no packing up at 3pm for them!

David John, Owie, Owen 'J', Margaret, Eleanor, Christine & Irene ready on the Maes to set off
on a day out to Rhyl. May 1953

Busy Maes – mid 20th Century (SWPC)

Memories… As you would expect, the centre of town was as busy on a Saturday night as it was during the day, with people out for an evening's entertainment at one of the three cinemas, out at the pub or even church. It was a place to see and be seen and by the mid 20th century Bertorelli's, the ice cream and tobacconist shop in the Square, had become the official start and stopping for a teenage social phenomenon known as the 'Turkey Trot' or 'Monkey Run'. This involved small groups of lads and small groups of girls each circling the town centre in opposite directions with the sole intention of interacting with the opposite sex. This was mainly a Saturday night event but was also repeated to a lesser extent on a Wednesday night (dydd Sadwrn bach). Eleanor Jones recalls that there wasn't much else to do for young people in the town at the time other than the Turkey Trot and the milk bars.

Eleanor and Margaret – teenage fun on the Maes near the Castle in 1952

Paternoster Buildings was without doubt one of the more handsome and aspirational buildings on the Maes, although these days it has lost the parapet and stone carved eagles which crown the top floor. The property was built by one time Victorian mayor of Caernarfon, Hugh Humphreys as his printing business expanded into bookselling and photography. Although the property was divided into sublets, he retained one part for himself, trading during the 1880s and 1890s as a portrait and landscape photographer. The name Paternoster is interesting for its link with Paternoster Row in London, which was the centre of the City's publishing trade until it was Blitzed in 1942. As this was also Mayor Humphrey's trade the link cannot be a coincidence.

Paternoster Buildings on the Maes c. 1930

By the time that this photograph was taken a Mr Williams had taken over the photography studio in the upstairs of the end part of Paternoster Buildings. Mr Williams' business cards indicate that he started his career on Merseyside and then later opened a branch here in Caernarfon on the High Street before moving to these prestigious premises on the Maes. Mr Williams's creative genes run strong in his descendents who are still photographing the town today.

To the left of the picture you can see that Bertorellis and Crosville were also established in Paternoster Buildings by this time. Directly below Mr Williams' studio you will see Aston's House Furnishers; a shop which was a solid feature of the square for over forty years. The liveried delivery vans that you can see in the picture were particularly important in an era before flat packed furniture allowed customers to transport it home themselves and even in fact before most people had their own motorised transport.

S. Aston & Son, House Furnishers. No. 14 Castle Square (Paternoster Buildings)

From the *Carnarvon & Denbigh Herald*, December 17th 1909:

"Before making their Xmas purchases, our readers will do well to glance down this column, and see what the best known establishments in the town have on sale, and what are the chief attractions in the windows ... At Messrs. Aston's well-known furnishing establishment the extensive display is as usual one of the most attractive in the town, the windows and first floor being devoted to a beautiful show of goods suitable for presentation. And from their useful and ornamental characters they are bound to be greatly appreciated by their recipients. The stock comprised all that is neatest, brightest, and prettiest in furnishing goods of every description. Apart from the very limited window space, the spacious and well-lighted showrooms are fitted with an immense stock of artistic and reliable goods of every description in the furnishing, ironmongery, drapery, and china and glass departments. Anyone contemplating furnishing or replenishing should inspect their immense stock. We would also remind our readers that all goods are manufactured at their new model factory at Wrexham, thus saving all middlemen's profits."

W. W. DAND
Gentlemen's Tailor and Outfitter
LADIES' DRESS SPECIALIST

FINE SELECTION OF VICUNAS, SERGES, AND HOMESPUNS

Castle Tailoring Establishment
CARNARVON

W. Wilson Dand, Gentlemen's Tailor and Outfitter, No. 20 Castle Square

During the 1930s The Maes (Castle Square) was home to Dand's Gentlemen's Tailor and Outfitter. No. 20 Castle Square had previously been the premises of E.H. Owen and Son, Auctioneers and Valuers and before that it had been a Music Warehouse run by Messrs Williams & Pritchard from around 1895. Earlier still, from the 1840s to the 1870s a Mr Peter Ellis had occupied it as a Grocer and Tea Dealer.

The Maes, Summer 1910, showing people and the odd vehicle gathered sociably around the fountain

A key feature of the Maes used to be the fountain which was built there and opened by Prince Edward of Wales in 1868. As with the buses it was a reason or a venue perhaps for people to congregate and this all added to the hustle and bustle and sheer sociability of the Maes. Today you'll find the remains of the fountain at the top of Pool Street where it forks off to Llanberis Road. Local people still miss this hub of the Maes.

Did you know? That the fountain was built as part of a new system of water works bringing fresh water to the town built following the cholera epidemic in the 1860s. This was a triumph for the efforts of the town's Mayor Sir Llewelyn Turner to improve the lot of the poor people of the town. It was obvious that poor sanitation was a public health hazard although science had not yet established exactly how or why. In fact a London-based doctor, Dr John Snow, had already publicised his theory of cholera being transmitted through the water supply but his theory had been rejected by the Government. It was only decades later that it was proved to be indisputably true.

CAERNARFON:
Market Town – County Town

One of the functions of a market and county town is to provide a centre for shopping. Not only at the actual market and market hall, but in the variety of shops that a town and its hinterland need. As we follow the photographers of yesteryear around the shopping streets of Caernarfon in the following pages, you will see that there was an almost infinite array of goods and services that could be found in the town – far more than we have today, when we often have to travel to out of town shopping centres or send for what we need by mail order.

The Maes – Market Day 1950s

Colin Jones recalls: "Harry Cross was a legendary stall holder on Caernarfon Square each Saturday, whose manual dexterity and non stop patter would enthral locals and visitors alike, as he sold his plates, bowls, cups and saucers. He had the ability to interlock a 21 piece tea set and display it in one hand - mind boggling!" [2]

Spotlight on High Street...

Caernarfon High Street census returns from 1891 tell us a great deal about the variety of people who lived on the street at the time, and the type of services that could be had there:

Premises	Head of Household	Age	Occupation
Custom House	George Challinor	30	Officer of Customs
SRW Yacht Club	William Tegarty	64	Army Pensioner
1 High Street	William Roberts	55	Licensed Victualler
(Public House *The Custom House Vaults*)			
2 High Street	Richard D Williams	48	Solicitor
3 High Street	Elizabeth R Williams	73	Private income
4 High Street	Ellen Jones	54	
	Hugh Jones	19	Fisherman
4 High Street	Ellen Roberts	52	
	John Roberts	21	Smith
	Llewelyn Roberts	16	Stone Mason
4 High Street	David Jones	47	Pilot
5 High Street	William Jones	82	Farmer (Retired)
6 High Street	Robert Williams	31	Bricklayer
7 High Street	Rose Ann Sadler	43	Confectioner
	Lucy Sneade	41	Confectioner
8 High Street	Owen Lloyd	44	Assistant Super of Prudential Assurance
9 High Street	Owen Roberts	55	Jeweller's Assistant
10 High Street	John Low	28	Publican
(Public House *The Snowdon Vaults*)			
11 High Street	John Jones	74	Licensed Victualler
(Public House *The Packet House*)			
12 High Street	Owen Jones	24	Grocer & Provision Dealer

13 High Street	Uriah Heard	51	Fishmonger
14 High Street	Mary Ellen Litherland	50	
	Thomas Litherland	21	Lithographer
	Fred Litherland	19	Lithographer
	Richard Litherland	16	Lithographer
15 High Street	Ann Jones	63	Grocer
17 & 19 High St.	Owen Jones	41	Licensed Victualler

(Public House *The Commercial* – today this is *The Crown*)

16 High Street	Griffith Davies	62	Master Mariner/ fishing boat owner
18 High Street	George Henry Heard	48	Fisherman
20 High Street	Edward Rowlands	71	Grocer
21 High Street	Richard Pritchard	36	Butcher
22 High Street	Robert F. Lightfoot	27	Publican
23 High Street	Evan Williams	42	Pork Butcher
24 High Street	Margaret Jones	62	Char-woman
26 High Street	William Lloyd	55	Chemist & Druggist
25 & 27 High St.	Mary Ann Owen	74	Chemist & Druggist
	William G Owen	40	Physician & Surgeon
	Griffith C Roose Owen	36	Chemist & Druggist
28 High Street	Alice Pritchard	31	Confectioner
29 High Street	Thomas Griffith	30	Grocer (Assistant)
34 High Street	William Knight	38	Shoe Maker
36 High Street	Edward Owen	35	Draper
35 High Street	John R Edwards	46	Printer & Publican
37 High Street	Robert Lloyd	46	China Dealer
39 High Street	William Roberts	63	Grocer (Master)
41 High Street	Thomas Davies	34	Seaman
41 High Street	Richard Williams	28	Seaman
41 High Street	Ellen Jones	66	Grocer

High Street

The High Street was once a major shopping street in the town which linked the shore-side west gate Porth yr Aur (Golden Gate) with the east gate Porth Mawr (Great Gate).

View of the busy High Street looking towards Porth Mawr and the Guildhall
astride the Gate, circa 1900

Did you know? That the Guildhall was originally the town's medieval Exchequer Office – the administrative and financial centre for Caernarfon, Anglesey and Merioneth. The building was adapted and changed several times during the eighteenth, nineteenth and twentieth centuries according to changing taste and intended use.

Just as today, premises changed hands and the names and use of the premises changed with it. Compare these photographs of the High Street taken about ten years after the 1891 census to see how the business names have changed.

This photograph taken around 1900 show No 29 High Street Thomas Lewis & Co and next door the tailor's shop owned by Messers Jones and Miller

On this side of the street we can clearly see that oysters were for sale, no doubt freshly caught by Caernarfon's fishermen – perhaps from the oyster bed established in 1897 on Caernarfon's foreshore by a Mr Lawson of Liverpool. Next door was a post office; the High Street post office (or stamp office) had been a fixture since at least 1844 if not earlier, but eventually small branches like these were replaced by the large post office on the Maes. Further along on the photograph, it's a little difficult to see, but the oil lamp fixed to the front of the building advertises 'The Adelphi Hotel' at No 34 High Street (Because of being on the street corner the Adelphi is also shown on the Census as No 1, Palace Street).

Eastgate Street

Eastgate Street early 20th century

A photographer looks back from Turf Square, along Eastgate Street towards Porth Mawr. (Through the arch is the High Street) It would seem from the deserted street and the closed shops that this photo was taken on a Sunday – the resulting image was used in a rather un–cheery Christmas card! Eastgate Street was home to the Carnarvon, Penygroes & District Co-operative Society – it first appears there in the Trade Directories in the 1920s and was still trading in the 1960s.

Bridge Street

Did you know? The name Bridge Street comes from the very origins of Edward I's medieval Caernarfon itself? The two rivers – Seiont and Cadnant made the location for Caernarfon a usefully defendable spot, cut off on three sides by water and overlooking the entrance to the Menai Strait. However, there were plenty of comings and goings to the new walled town and castle, which required relatively easy access to the town. To resolve this a dam known as 'Great Bridge' was created to facilitate traffic into the town.

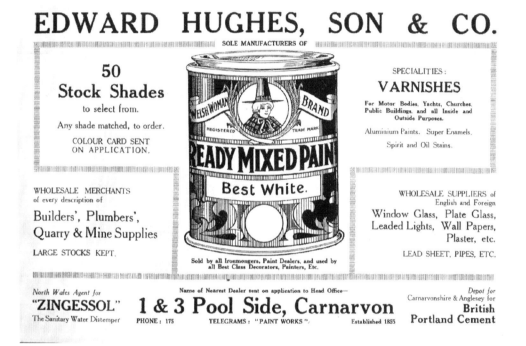

Bridge Street – Edward Hughes & Son Ironmongers on the corner of Bridge Street and Pool Side (Penllyn)

In November 1897 Edward Hughes, Ironmonger, displayed his finest wares at the Industrial Trade, Food, and Sanitary Appliances Exhibition held at Caernarfon's Pavilion. (Of which, more later). The Carnarvon and Denbigh Herald reported on 26th November that he had a "fine show of incandescent lights, cooking ranges, and gas stoves, tile grates, and mantel pieces, tile hearths, and wood, iron, and enamel chimney pieces, all forming a very pretty sight." The paper also reported that a great many Cofis had attended the exhibition which pleased the promoters because "the object of the exhibition was to introduce to [the town] some of the most important domestic appliances and to do good to the trade of the town" The reporter added his own "(hear, hear)" to this sentiment.

*Bridge Street: The lighter coloured building towards the end of the row was the Nelson Emporium.
Photograph taken circa 1900*

The Nelson Emporium after the 1992 fire

Memories ... children of the town wondered sadly whether the large 'Silentnight' toy hippo had escaped the blaze at the Nelson Emporium. His fate is not recorded...

Possibly the most well known shop on Bridge Street was the Nelson Emporium. In the 1920s Nelsons advertised themselves "as the largest drapery establishment and the most comprehensive stock in North Wales, Noted for Coats, Frocks and Millinery, Ladies' and Children's Outfitters and Dainty Hosiery", and in December the lengthy queues of parents and excited children waiting to visit Nelson's Father Christmas stretched right down the street.

In 1948 the Nelson Emporium fell victim to fire, devastating the Victorian three storey building. But ever keen to continue trading, a new premises was built on the corner of Bridge Street and Pool Side where the ironmongers had been, and where Dodrefyn Perkins (Furniture) is now in 2010. The replacement premises traded for over forty years, still a staple feature of the town, but bad luck returned to haunt the owners when the new store too burnt down in 1992. Nelson's was no more.

Bridge Street: Harpers Restaurant

In the 1950s Harpers Restaurant on Bridge Street was a smart venue, fashionable with wedding parties and both Margaret and Hazel Parry had their wedding breakfasts here. Looking at this photograph taken after her wedding, Margaret remembers that Harpers was a very popular place to go for your wedding breakfast and other special occasions in those days. Upstairs (at street level) it was a cake shop on one side of the double front and a cigarette shop on the other side. The Restaurant was downstairs where the Parry girls and their new husbands celebrated their marriages with their families and friends.

Pool Street

Pool Street from the Maes end. (Late 1920s/early 1930s)

Our photographer here seems to have captured Pool Street on just an ordinary shopping day – a delivery of large bales and barrels has arrived by cart outside the wholesalers, a gentleman is descending a ladder at the front of the shop next door to the café perhaps having made repairs or cleaned windows, a man in a classic bowler hat stands outside the bank (then the Bank of England, currently Natwest). Interestingly, the ladies walking briskly up the street are universally blurry apart from their ankles, twinkling clearly below their coats in what was then still a very modern style of dress.

Pool Street from the top looking down (Edwardian period)

In the foreground of the Pool Street photo a bunch of children lark about, excited by the unusual presence of a photographer. The two buildings on the right with the lower roof lines are no more, having been replaced by the (former) Woolworths building in 1930 and later the Boots Chemist building next door. Evan Owen's Bakery, where you can see the staff standing at the door, is today a hardware shop, part of the local Stermat chain.

The Continental Milk Bar 1962 – brothers Luigi and Dorino Miserotti serving customers in their Pool Street cafe (Pic: National Library of Wales)

The Continental Milk Bar was opened in Pool Street in 1936 by Luigi and Dorino Miserotti's parents. They were fresh from Italy via Aberystwyth. They worked long hours six days a week and eventually Luigi and Dorino took over, keeping the café kept going right through until 1986. Milk Bars had been spreading rapidly all over Britain since the early 1930s and the first National Milk Bar had been established in Colwyn Bay in 1933.

In the 1950s and 1960s milk bars became very fashionable – it was well known that The Beatles frequented a milk bar in Lime Street (Liverpool) – and this probably accounts for the fact that Caernarfon could support a number of such popular establishments. The milk bars became a staple part of the 'Turkey Trot' routine on a Saturday night.

The ultimate in long-running shops in Caernarfon has to be the jewellers
Roberts & Owen in Pool Street (Gwynedd Archives Service)

Originally 12 Pool Street was the premises of John Hughes, watchmaker and jeweller from before 1840 until his death in 1863. The business was preserved by his widow in partnership with Robert Roberts and, on the death of John's widow, Robert Roberts and Evan Owen joined together as Roberts and Owen.

Roberts and Owen continues to sell jewellery at 12 Pool Street today in 2010.

Did you know? The pool after which the Pool-Side area is named was created by the medieval Great Bridge restricting the flow of the Cadnant. The dam made a pool which powered two medieval water mills.

Kenrick Evans tells us that "The Pool was drained about the middle of the nineteenth century by dumping the town rubbish on either side of the Cadnant stream; when a width of six to eight feet had been reached, the stream (open) was provided with stone walling."[3]

It wasn't until some time later that the stream was covered over completely. The area was still prone to flooding however. The Cadnant was not so easily subdued and made its presence felt on many occasions.

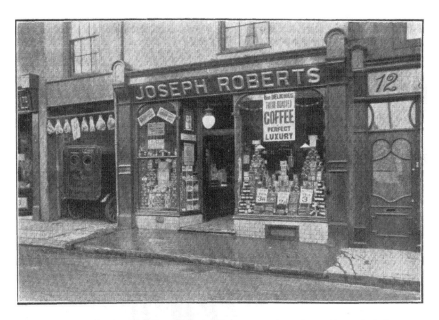

JOSEPH ROBERTS

Wholesale and Retail

GROCER AND

Italian Warehouseman

The well-known County Tea Warehouse

14 Pool St. & Twthill Tea Mart

CARNARVON

TELEPHONE 87

Joseph Roberts, Grocer at No. 14 Pool Street

Next door to Roberts and Owen was Joseph Roberts, the well known grocer who had two premises in the town; this one here in the centre and the other up in the Twthill residential area. The Twthill branch specialised in Tea ('The County Tea Warehouse'), but here in town the speciality was Italian products and he advertises himself as an Italian Warehouseman. Shops like these sold imported products such as pasta, olive oil, pickles, perfumes, fruits, paints and pigments, in addition to the more general grocery products.

T. E. GRIFFITH

MEAT PURVEYOR

**Best Welsh Meat Only.
Welsh Mutton a Speciality.
NO Foreign.**

26 Pool Street, Carnarvon

TELEPHONE No. 58

T.E. Griffith, Family Butcher at No. 26 Pool Street

A little further up the road was Griffith's butchers. Today we would be surprised to see meat hanging outside the shop like this, but this photograph was taken during the 1930s when butchers could still enjoy this centuries-old way of displaying their wares. Now of course, hygiene regulations would forbid it! In his advert Mr Griffith stresses that he sold only Welsh meat and NO foreign products. Despite steam ships bringing refrigerated lamb and so on to the UK from places like New Zealand, food miles were generally much less of an issue in those days for fresh produce, especially in rural market towns like Caernarfon. The meat for sale here in this picture most likely having been brought in from local farms to the slaughter house in Victoria Dock and bought by Mr Griffith and his fellow butchers in Caernarfon.

A NIGHT ON THE TOWN

We are so used to our home entertainments now that it's hard for the reader born after the 1950s to imagine a time when there was no television (or only limited channels), and certainly no computers, internet, PlayStations or Wii. Home entertainment before these technological innovations might have involved a radio ('wireless'), music, reading and 'parlour' or board games, depending on the family's preference or income. But there wasn't the variety of streamed entertainment that we can get in our homes today and to get that the Cofis of yesteryear had to go out into their town.

The Guildhall seems to have been the first specific entertainment venue in Caernarfon. In the 1860s audiences could enjoy such delights as music recitals, poetry readings, ventriloquism and conjuring, and later in the century 'living pictures' or 'tableau vivant' where actors and actresses posed in scenes from famous paintings which were then 'brought to life'. At the end of the Great War in 1918 a poignant Tableau Vivant was shown at the Guild Hall in commemoration of those who had lost their lives. Other events were more lively and on 17th June 1865 the *Carnarvon & Denbigh Herald* reported on a popular act at the Guildhall:

"SIGNOR BOSCO AT THE GUILDHALL The well known ventriloquist and conjurer Signor Bosco, gave one of his celebrated entertainments at the Guildhall on Tuesday evening last, under the patronage of the Mayor, Llewelyn Turner, Esq., to a large and enthusiastic audience. A series of tricks, illusions, &c., including the rope tying feat, were performed and evoked much applause. The performance concluded with the trick in firing a plate against the wall. And the audience after a séance of two hours were permitted to disperse like Oliver Twist with an appetite for more."

'Signor' Leotard Bosco

The Pavilion

Caernarfon with Pavilion in foreground circa 1920.

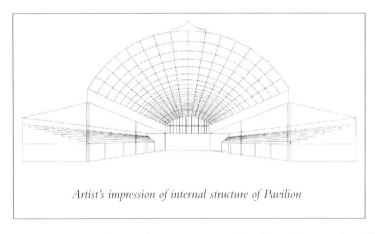

Artist's impression of internal structure of Pavilion

Behind the castle is the rise of the hill at Coed Helen and the summer house at its peak. The other great place of live indoor entertainment in Caernarfon in the nineteenth and twentieth centuries was the Pavilion. The site of this once grand edifice is now home to the local Welsh National Assembly and local government offices behind the town library and is commemorated in the road name Lôn Pafiliwn.

All over the UK at this time, town authorities in holiday resorts, were investing in these 'palaces of pleasure' to provide a venue for every type of indoor event whatever the weather. Caernarfon was not slow in following suit and in 1877 the Pavilion was under construction at the same time as Blackpool was investing in its own pleasure palace, the Winter Gardens. No one could call the Pavilion beautiful, with its corrugated iron roof and brick and glass sports-hall-meets-airplane-hanger external appearance, but as the largest public hall in Wales of its day seating up to 8,000 people, my goodness was it a useful space!

In September 1895 the Pavilion hosted a 'Grand Bazaar' depicting Constantinople to be held in aid of clearing a debt of £4,000 on the organ and schoolrooms at Moriah Chapel (Gwynedd Archives Service)

A poster for the Grand Bazaar advertised that a kinetoscope (a device for viewing moving pictures) and phonograph (like a gramophone) to be seen as well. No doubt long queues formed to see these two items which represented the latest in entertainment technology. Today we might liken it to going into an Apple store to test out an iPad for the first time – something which future readers will probably find equally antiquated! In 1895, visitors to the Grand Bazaar were treated to live music by the Band of the Royal Marine Light Infantry.

£4,000 was not an inconsiderable amount to be raising, but even so the work which must have gone into creating the scenery is amazing. Our Victorian forebears didn't do things by halves! Behind the Constantinople scenery there were side aisles with inward-facing tiered seating, and as you can see the central hall was open to the roof allowing for a myriad of uses. The height of the building even allowed for an act where a lady was winched up to the ceiling and drifted down by parachute to the floor!

Tables and chairs, stages, scenery, dancing, exhibits, war-time stores – all could be and were accommodated in the Pavilion during the next eighty or so years. From local uses, such as the Church Bazaars, to well known and much-anticipated entertainers, politicians such as David and Megan Lloyd George and the great non-conformist preachers – all held the Caernarfon audiences in their thrall here at the Pavilion. The national Eisteddfod was held in the Pavilion five times before the Government commandeered the building during the second war. The Government lease ran right up to 1956, after which time the condition of the building was so poor that despite protests it was eventually pulled down.

David Lloyd George speaks to the crowds in Caernarfon Pavilion (Gwynedd Archives Service)

At the other end of its life the Pavilion looks sad and forgotten in this photograph taken at the time of its demolition in 1962

In October 1961, Caernarfon said goodbye to its Pavilion after nearly one hundred years. A special farewell concert was arranged by the BBC and was broadcast live on the radio. Cofis and aficionados filling the hall for the last time were treated to music, hymn singing and speeches and sermons from the past greats such as David Lloyd George and the preacher Christmas Evans. By the end of the evening there was not a dry eye in the house.

Those readers who want to experience this moment, or relive it, should visit the Gwynedd Archives Service at Victoria Dock and ask to listen to the two reels XD1/1146 and XD1/1147.

Eisteddfodau

A little background for the uninitiated – essentially an Eisteddfod is a Welsh language festival of literature, poetry, music and song overseen by a community or *gorsedd* of Bards. (Eisteddfodau is the plural). Many Welsh places hold their own local Eisteddfod, but each August a National Eisteddfod is held, alternating in venue between North and South Wales.

Proclamation of the National Eisteddfod 1905 in Caernarfon Castle

In the previous section I referred to the five national Eisteddfodau held in Caernarfon Pavilion before the Second World War and the Government took over the premises. The events, concerts and competitions of the Eisteddfod were held in the Pavilion in 1886, then 1894, 1906, 1921 and finally 1935. However it was the dramatic setting of Caernarfon's Castle that the Bards turned to in 1905 to declare the 1906 Eisteddfod. Tradition dictates that the intention to stage an Eisteddfod must be announced at least one year and a day before the actual event. This photograph shows the Gorsedd of the Bards at the 1905 Proclamation Ceremony in Caernarfon Castle. During the ceremony a bard elected as the Recorder reads the Proclamation Scroll and the list of competitions for the following year's National Eisteddfod is presented to the Archdruid.

A year later in 1906 the National Eisteddfod came to Caernarfon. Crowds line the streets to watch the procession of the Bards and other dignitaries leaving the Gorsedd in the Castle to begin the proceedings at the Pavilion

Choirs

Leading naturally on from the subject of Eisteddfod has to be of course the thing that people always associate with the Welsh – singing!

Amassed choirs entertaining the Royal party and guests at the 1911 investiture of Prince Edward of Wales at Caernarfon Castle

This close-up shows that the gentlemen were in suits and straw boaters but the ladies were in traditional Welsh costume

Caernarfon Choral Society singing in the Castle, conducted by Mr J. Williams and accompanied by Mr W. Morris. In their inaugural year the Caernarfon Choral Society won the Chief Choral Competition at the 1909 National Eisteddfod held in London. The Society ran until 1930 and had nearly two hundred members

Saturday Night at the Movies...

Even as early as the first decade of the1900s such live entertainment as was provided at the Pavilion and the Guildhall was rivalled by the new medium of film. At one time Caernarfon boasted three cinemas – one in the Guildhall, the Empire and the Majestic.

The Guildhall started showing films before 1910, calling itself the Guild Hall Picture Palace

By 1910 the Guildhall could sit up to 500 cinema-goers at a time to watch the synchronised gramophone 'talkies' and the famous bi-weekly newsreel the *Pathe Gazette*.

Guild Hall Picture Palace,

Nightly, 7.30 to 10.   Saturday, 2.30 & 7.30.

Mon., Tues., and Weds. :--

Tragedies of Crystal Globe,

Featuring MABEL TRUNNELLE.   :::   3 REEL DRAMA.

Thurs., Fri., and Sat. :--

"The House of Lost Court,"

Featuring GERTRUDE McCOY.   ✶-✶   5 REEL DRAMA.

:: The Best Show in Carnarvon. ::

In 1915 the Guild Hall Picture Palace was showing these two silent movies

THE MAJESTIC CINEMA, CAERNARVON

★ TEL.. 16      TEL.. 16 ★

Best in Sound, Picture and Comfort.

*THE MAJESTIC will open on Monday next (August Bank Holiday) but the Official Civic Opening
will be performed by the Mayor of Caernarfon (Councillor W.G.Williams) the following Saturday,
August 11th. Capt. Pritchard has, on the suggestion of the Mayor kindly promised to allot the proceeds
of the Matinee on Saturday, to the funds of the Caernarvon Cottage Hospital.*

GREAT OPENING WEEK ATTRACTIONS

MONDAY , AUGUST 6th

BANK HOLIDAY
FOR THREE DAYS

JESSIE MATTHEWS, SONNIE HALE,
AND
BETTY BALFOUR
IN

EVERGREEN

LAVISHLY PRODUCED AND BRILLIANTLY ACTED STORY OF A
MUSIC HALL STAR'S TRIUMPH
Cert" A"

THURSDAY, AUGUST 9th

FOR THREE DAYS
SONNIE HALE, GWYNETH LLOYD,
FLANNAGHAN AND ALLEN
- IN -

WILD BOY

A DELIGHTFUL BRITISH COMEDY DRAMA WITH GREYHOUND
RACING AS PICTURESQUE AND EXITING BACKGROUND.
"U"

Daily at 6pm, and 8-30pm Matinee Daily 2-30 at Reduced Prices. Admission Prices : Balcony 2/- and 1/6; Stalls, 1/3 and 1/- (including Tax)
AIDS TO HEARING: This Theatre is equipped with Special Ear Phones for the convenience of Deaf Patrons. NO EXTRA CHARGE.

The Majestic advertises its opening day, bank holiday Monday 6th August 1934

Empire Picture Palace Films still lacked integral soundtracks when Mr Caradoc Rowlands opened the Empire Picture Palace in 1915 but in the 1930s both cinemas had British Acoustic sound systems installed to allow them to show the new style films with sound – 'the talkies'. It was the talkies which really got people obsessed with going to the cinema and demand for seats grew hugely. So it should come as no surprise then that a third cinema was built in Caernarfon on Bangor Street opening on the bank holiday 6th August 1934 – the Majestic Cinema.

The New Majestic Cinema was built in the modern Art Deco style with the latest sound system and boasted one large screen (nearly the size of a double decker bus), with seating for 1,050 patrons! Older readers will recall on seeing the advert how there used to be a range of prices depending on the seats you sat in, unlike today. The cinema was built with a snack bar upstairs to encourage people to make it a sociable evening or afternoon out. As with most cinemas at the time, only having the one screen meant that the manager would change the film being shown half way through the week to encourage people to come more than once.

In the 1950s Margaret Parry and her sister Hazel worked at the Majestic Cinema as smartly attired usherettes.

The staff from both the Empire (then known as the Caernarfon Playhouse) and Majestic Cinemas together with their manager Mr Morgan. (Hazel Parry is third from right on the top row)

The Majestic Snack Bar had been renamed the Majestic Milk Bar in keeping with the trend of the 1950s. The two cinemas, Majestic and Empire, had come into the ownership of Guy Bakers Paramount Picture Theatres Ltd after the war and in 1956 both were fitted with the new Cinemascope system to improve the audience experience. With the two purpose built cinemas in Caernarfon offering such an up-to-date experience, it is not surprising that the Guildhall was shut down two years later.

Margaret Parry with some of her colleagues outside the Majestic From left to right: Margaret,
Len Westlake, David Jones & Bob Jones (Lan-Mor)

Autumn 1964 Remembrance Sunday (?) Parade passing the
Majestic 1964

In 1964 the Majestic was showing an obscure British horror film called the Black Torment – this backdrop of entertainment contrasts with the Remembrance Day (?) parade passing by and the dignitaries taking the salute on the steps of the cinema. The other two cinemas survived as picture palaces until the 1970s & 80s when the Empire saw the rise of bingo start to take over, and the Majestic, which had been showing live entertainment such as wrestling in addition to films, was transformed into a night club.

'A Northern Soul All Dayer' was promised here at the Majestic on August bank holiday 1981

By this time the Majestic was no longer promoting itself as a cinema, and had begun to call itself the Canolfan Adloniant Majestic (The Majestic Entertainment Centre). Northern Soul (for those too young to remember) was a dance and music phenomenon which evolved out of the black American soul music Tamla Motown in Northern England in the late 1960s. The movement reached a peak of popularity in the 1970s and in North Wales the focus for Northern Soul was Llandudno at Paynes Cafe Royal. But this music had its fans in the other towns too and in 1981 Cel Thomas and John Parry persuaded Mike King, the owner, to let them stage a twelve hour event at the Majestic.

Originally they had hoped for an 'all nighter' but had to settle for an 'all dayer' instead. The poster on the photograph advertises a Guest DJ for its Caernarfon Soulers – this was none other than Pat Brady who had headlined at all the top Northern Soul venues over the past decade. Although Cel remembers that a good time was had by those that turned up, the turnout was disappointing overall, suggesting that Northern Soul hadn't boogied its way down the coast and won the hearts and feet of the Cofis. The Majestic's wrestling nights with the popular wrestlers of the day like Billy Two Rivers and Giant Haystacks and local bands entertaining in the intervals had been more popular in this town!

The Majestic evolves with the times; 'Fun Pubs' were all the rage in the early 1990s

The Entertainment Centre had evolved with the times and functioned as a fun pub and then a nightclub called The Dome before being closed in the early nineties. Fun pubs revolutionised nights out for the young at the end of the 1980s and usually went in for trendy lighting, loud music, fancy drinks and often some kind of live entertainment or theme nights too – blurring the distinction between pubs and nightclubs, and definitely moving as far away as possible from the traditional pub. Shortly after this photograph was taken in 1993 the Majestic fell victim to arson and the venue was demolished.

Outdoor Pursuits *(for those who didn't want to climb every mountain...)*

For the more outdoorsy types, Caernarfon offered a variety of attractions. Caernarfon Park was opened in May 1844 by the squire of Faenol, Thomas Assheton Smith

A leaflet from 1909 declares that "It may be said that the Caernarvon folk esteem their Public Park with a large degree of pride ... [it is] diverse in character and very tastefully laid out with choice shrubberies, rustic bridges, and miniature cascades flowing to and from the lake which is an ornamental feature in the centre". Visitors to the park could play cricket, football and bowls there and "ample provision is made for romping ground for juveniles".[4]

Caernarfon Municipal Recreation Grounds

At the front of the Pavilion was the Municipal Recreation Grounds which offered tennis and bowls as this advert from the 1930s shows. Much further back in time to the eighteenth century Caernarfon residents played the old game of Fives in this area, where a ball is hit against a wall with bare hands – a bit like an extreme version of squash!

Caernarfon's Sea Water Bathing Pool on the Aber Foreshore, 1930s

The Victorians and Edwardians were great believers in the powers of sea water and so it follows that in 1905 Caernarfon should have had its own sea water bathing pool on the Aber Foreshore near where the football training ground is now on the edge of the Strait. These chaps from 1933 look determined to enjoy themselves despite the disadvantages of woollen bathing suits, the icy tidal waters and the sealife lurking in the corners below the feet of the swimmers. Judging by the shallowness of the water, the tide which filled the pool must have been low!

CARNARVON OPEN-AIR SEA WATER SWIMMING BATH.

DELIGHTFUL BATHING AT ALL HOURS OF THE DAY.

DIVISION OF DAY AND TARIFF.			
HOURS . . .	6 a.m. to 10 a.m.	10 a.m to 12 noon	After 12 noon.	After 6 p.m.
BATHERS . .	Gentlemen only.	Ladies only.	Mixed.	Mixed.
CHARGES . .	3d. each.	3d. each.	3d. each.	1d. each.

EXTRA CHARGES : *Use of Towel, 1d. ; Use of Costume, 1d.*
SPECIAL TERMS FOR SCHOOLS.

Pool opening times and prices

Memories of the sea water bathing pool…

Generations of children learned to swim here and Colin Jones recalls his memories of the pool in the 1950s:

"[Here I learned the] rudiments of swimming and life saving under the watchful eye of Mr. Will. Pritchard (Welsh Guards) whose word was law and evenhandedness a by-word… The pool itself was a Victorian edifice, crescent shaped and 80yards in length. It was filled by tidal flow and the depth of water within depended to a great extent on the height of the tides in the straits. In the early days it boosted a rickety diving board (later replaced by a safer one) and an infamous "greasy pole". This piece of emasculating appendage consisted of a wooden ship's mast wedged horizontally into one of the overflow ports in the wall of the pool at about three feet above water level. The challenge being to be able to walk along this 15 foot pole successfully and diving off the end. It remained a constant source of hilarity as participants lost balance, with often devastating results, which they invariably tried to mask when eventually surfacing.

In my early days at Caernarfon baths as they were known, there was little or no filtration of the water as it entered via the inlet pipe from the sea and often one could find crabs, shrimp and blennies abounding in the recesses of the 'deep end'. Chlorination did not arrive until the late 50's and there were often cases of severe eye irritation as the incumbent bath manager tried to stabilize the flow of added chlorine to acceptable levels. I still pause and view the vestiges of this haven of schoolboy memories as I walk the foreshore now and recall myriads of happy days." [5]

To get to the sea water bathing pool one had to cross the river Seiont via the swing bridge. Locals call it *dros yr aber* or 'over the aber' – the aber being the mouth of the river.

In 1953 Eleanor and the girls pose on the Aber Foreshore side with the old swing bridge and its watch tower in the back ground. (Oh yes, and the castle of course!)

The original swing bridge had been opened by the town council in 1899 and was maintained by them for many years. However, with safety in mind, the bridge had to be closed in 1963 to vehicles and in 1967 to pedestrians. Eventually it was removed and when the Investiture of Prince Charles as Prince of Wales took place in 1969 a temporary bridge had to be erected for the event. This was not retained and it took another six years for the new Aber Bridge to be constructed and opened to people crossing over the river to the Aber Foreshore.

This photograph shows the period in the early 1970s between the old bridge being taken down and the new bridge being erected, when people wishing to cross the river had to go all the way round via the Seiont Bridge

View of Coed Helen and the Aber Foreshore circa 1910

The Aber Foreshore was a place of recreation where people could promenade on a nice day as they do now, or play and paddle in the water of the river mouth, an activity which has waned in popularity over the past half century. (Were we hardier in those days?)

Mr Baggby's Snack Van on the Aber Foreshore in the 1970s

In the 1960s a new restaurant opened in Caernarfon, Lee Ho's famous floating restaurant, moored near the Anglesey Arms hotel on the Promenade

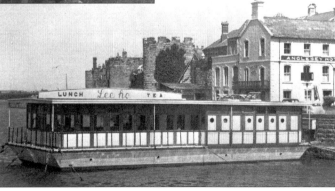

The annual Regatta on the Menai Strait in 1908

If you had not crossed the river, but walked around the Castle the other way, you would find yourself in the 'South of France' – the local name for this stretch which despite its openness the to Strait is a good place to find and enjoy the sun and the views. Here (near the Anglesey Arms) you would have once found Caernarfon's Medieval quay but by the 1800s this walk had been firmly established as a promenade and in 1813 *The Cambrian Tourist Guide and Companion* described it in glowing terms:

"A wide terrace extending from the quay to the north end of the town walls, forms a most charming walk, the fashion-able promenade, in fine weather, for all descriptions of people, who, while they inhale the salubrious breeze, may be agreeably amused by the moving varieties of the port."

DOWN TO BUSINESS

Life is not all beer and skittles, as they say, and some of the economic spirit and energy of Caernarfon's industrial past is captured here on film.

SLATE QUAY

This early photograph shows merchant ships docked at the harbour in 1864. At this time the north-west Wales slate industry was at its peak of production and despatch to all four corners of the industrialising world. However, ships also brought all kinds of goods into the town – Joseph Roberts' Italian grocery products perhaps?

The river mouth of the Seiont makes a natural harbour in 1864 at the height of the slate trade

Segontium Terrace can be seen on its low cliff overlooking the river at the far centre-left point of the picture

Slate Quay on the banks of the Seiont just past the Castle (below Segontium Terrace)

The Slate Quay fronting on to the mouth of the River Seiont is now around 200 years old and this photograph shows it still functioning as a working quay despatching ships loaded with locally produced products all around the world.

In the centre of the photograph you can see the buildings of the Union/de Wintons ironworks; the tallest building was the foundry's erecting shed through which passed girders for the Houses of Parliament and components for the Britannia Bridge, as well as specialist equipment for the slate industry up in the mountains and quarries above the town. The premises included "offices, stores, erecting shop, fitting and turning shop, foundry and boiler shop; there was also a pattern shop and a large yard beyond, with a smithy and timber stocks." [6] De Wintons was a thriving business with many employees and even their own football team in the second half of the nineteenth century but by the end of the century Lewis Lloyd concludes that "they seem to have overreached themselves in respect of over-ambitious contracts, which required considerable capital expenditure". [7]

To the front of the photograph below are the buildings and yards of Slate Quay itself, built by the Caernarfon Harbour Company in response to the increasing importance of the slate industry in the world market. Individual slate quarry owners could lease an area of the Quay for storage and embarkation of their product.

Rail trucks (seen on the far right of the picture) brought slate down from the quarries to Slate Quay

This peaceful looking photograph of Slate Quay in 1946 with no merchant ships indicates the struggle of the slate quarrying industry, the rise of road and rail haulage and the beginning of the town's slide into reliance on the tourist trade as a main source of revenue

Victoria Dock

Low tide at Victoria dock

Around the other side of the Castle, a new dock, known first as New Basin (later Victoria Dock) was dug in 1868 at the point where the river called Cadnant empties out its mountain water into the Menai Strait. As this photograph shows it was no exclusive marina when it was built – these are working boats, very different from the vessels that dock there today.

Norman Phillips recalls the black smelly alluvial mud which the Cadnant also brought down with it into the dock giving work to a large dredger named the Seiont Two. This has now been alleviated by the introduction of a sluice gate in recent times.

Keeping the Victoria Dock clear of silt – a job for the Seiont II

Victoria Mill towards the end of its life in the latter part of the twentieth century. (The small crane at the far left of the photograph is still on the dock at the side of Y Harbwr Pub.)

In 1899 this building was the premises of the millers W. Pritchard and was known as Victoria Mill. Later it was taken over by North Shore Mill Co Ltd., listed in the trade directory in 1936. Grain dust is a very combustible substance and the mill was the scene of a great fire in 1910 after which its owners were at great pains to reassure their customers that their orders would be fulfilled as usual. The postcards issued to this effect do not explain exactly how this would be achieved!

A variety of businesses throughout the years used the Victoria Dock for their location. The nineteenth century saw the dockside buildings and warehousing develop; a timber yard, used for the storage of timber imported from America, a slaughter house and the corn mill were established, amongst others.

This photographer has captured the final operational years of a Victoria Dock where working boats still drop anchor and businesses still function in the dock buildings and warehouses. At the far side the Esso and Shell Petrol Depot silos dominate the horizon

Not just the preserve of warehouses, the docks became a place for any business that might want to export their products, or even just serve Caernarfon in the case of the Modernist-style Electricity Works. Local people still recall with fondness the Corona Factory, the abbatoir (mainly interesting to small boys with noses pressed to the mesh trying to see in!) and the Corset Factory, which took over the Electricity Works building after the Second World War when Caernarfon was promoting itself as a location for light industry. There were far fewer 'food-miles' in those days – the animals for slaughter at the abbatoir had come from local farms, to the cattle market at Gipsy Hill in the town, thence to the slaughter house and from there the meat went to Caernarfon's butchers and the hides to the tannery on the Llanberis Road.

The slate merchant, Fletcher and Dixon, had a good write-up in a post-war promotional pamphlet, where it was noted that they were an old established firm making items from small whetstones to large brewery fermenting vessels, as well as more standard slate building requirements. Additionally they were "practically the sole world producers of slate billiard beds" and slate electrical switchboard bases for electrical construction firms". [8]
On a lighter note, Victoria Dock (given to glorious sunsets) was a favourite place for courting couples. (Another source of fascination to the local children!).

This panorama of the docks taken in the 1980s shows how built up Victoria Dock became over the decades. Ex-postman David Williams has identified the buildings for us

1 – Slipway for ferry to Anglesey   5 – Corset Factory
2 – Corona Factory   6 – Fletcher and Dixon Slate Merchant
3 – Ships' Pilot   7 – Esso and Shell Petrol Depot
4 – Distribution Centre

The Salmon Fishermen

Of course the Strait wasn't just a sea-going highway, a very special group of Cofis worked on the Strait itself – they were the salmon fishermen.

Dafydd Ellis recalls his days as a netsman fondly: "Locals and visitors would spend all the tide just watching the salmon fishermen and listening to the jokes and leg pulling from the crew… I spent 25 best years of my life fishing the Menai Straits and so did a lot of others".

June 1933, John Lovell, a fisherman from Mountain Street and his crew of three, caught a record catch of salmon in the Menai Strait

David Williams (whose uncle W. Williams took the photo) recalls the tale of that day for us in June 1933: "Lovell's crew were fishing with a net in the early morning in the vicinity of the public baths when they had a haul of 41 salmon, weighing about 700 pounds. Owing to the low water in the river Seiont, salmon had been plentiful in the Menai Straits and John Lovell and his crew had already had a total catch of over 100 salmon, weighing nearly 1,500 pounds, during that season.

It is thought that the previous record catch was made over forty years

On 14th July 1963 Mr W.M. Jones's (Will Bee) salmon fishing boat had just docked at the dock entrance when this photograph was taken

previously, when a boat known locally as *'Cwch Salvation'* had a haul of between 500–600 pounds."
Left to right, the 1963 crew were composed of: Doug Lovell leaning on the rail, in the background was Guto Da Da, (as he was known), then skipper Will Bee. Looking down at the catch was Emrys ' Snails' and then last but not least, Norman Bohana. Although there were seven boats operating from the dock at one time you won't see salmon fishermen working the Strait today; a lack of salmon forced the last Caernarfon netsman Robert Watkinson, to give up operating as a commercial business in 1997.

The Staff of the Brick Works in 1940

Factories and offices

Of course, not every workplace in Caernarfon was about heavy industry. We have peeked down the streets of Caernarfon's yesteryear, and looked into some of the shop windows. But what about the people who worked there? The census from the High Street suggests that at the turn of the twentieth century people often lived above or behind the shop or office where they worked – even in the case of the old Nelson Emporium, where a whole clutch of drapery assistants and a cook lived above the store. But usually not everyone could live 'over the shop' and it's said locally that by the mid twentieth century a kind of precedent had established itself whereby the girls from the surrounding villages worked in the shops and the girls from the town worked in factories like the corset factory. Other factories in the town included the Corona Factory, the Compact Factory (making compacts for ladies face powder), the Tannery on Llanberis Road which stank out the immediate area and a multitude of others smaller and larger in and around the town.

Between Caernarfon Park and Peblig Mill was Caernarfon's brick works. Probably many local readers will recognise relatives amongst this photograph, but even if you don't the picture is interesting for its more unusual characters such as the dog, the very smiley lady in the middle, and the chaps we must assume are the management in their smart outfits. The gentleman in the middle with the apron and the rolled up shirt sleeves looks like he must be the foreman of this crew, with his tie and waistcoat under his apron suggesting his seniority.

After the war the Hunting Aviation workshops at Peblig Mill went on to be used for a variety of manufacturing purposes including the manufacture of aluminium and plastic bedroom furniture called Basildon 'New Period'.

A Basildon 'New Period' cabinet being constructed at Peblig Mill in 1947

Another company that traded at Peblig Mill in the early postwar period was Bernard Wardle's Everflex Factory. Opening in 1948 to manufacture pvc leathercloth for car interiors and the like, Everflex at its peak of manufacture employed 800 staff, making it the largest concern in the area. It was a devastating blow

therefore, when the Caernarfon branch of this company was closed in 1980 despite the efforts of a local action committee and demonstrations in the town to try to reverse the decision. Such a blow was this that the MP Dafydd Wigley even brought it up at the House of Commons in the spring of that year. All to no avail. [9]

Everflex factory floor during the early years of manufacture at Peblig Mill. This photograph of Arwyn Roberts and his colleagues seems to capture just an ordinary day at work in the early 1950s

During the war Hunting Aviation had also used the old Electricity Works on Victoria Dock as a machine shop, and this property was released by the Government after the War to be used by private industry again – becoming the Corset Factory.

Margaret, Nellie, Eleanor and Irene getting some fresh air on the dock in their lunch break from the corset factory, 1953

These girls were just four of the hundred or so workers who were employed in this "most modern and healthy factory, equipped with the latest machinery" for corsetry.[10] Eleanor Jones recalls that working on the machines was a good, clean job to have and she worked there happily for nine years until she married.

Taken in the latter part of the twentieth century, this photograph shows the demolition of the William Champness & Sons' Corset factory in progress

Being the County Town has meant that Caernarfon has always required administrators, solicitors, accountants and clerks of all kinds. Their workplaces tend not to generate photographs so this photograph is quite unusual. The piles of files in the background serves as a reminder of how much paper filing we had to do before computers did it for us – and how accurate we had to be with the filing systems. Oh the horror of desperately searching for a mis-filed set of accounts!

Front row, third from left is Miss Violet Annie Roberts who worked for the Council from the end of WW1 up until reaching her retirement in 1960, by which time she was a head of department. This was probably her retirement photograph as she kept it safe amongst her possessions.

Office workers in Caernarfon, 1960

CHANGING TOWN

Pool Side / Penllyn before and during demolition

Towns change all the time. Often it's in subtle ways that imperceptibly impact on our lives, bit by bit so that we don't notice it happening. Other times it's a huge wrench to lose something – especially a place where townsfolk have done a lot of living like a school or a hospital. From as early as 1915 Carnarvon Corporation started a process of demolishing houses deemed not fit for habitation. This continued between the wars and the need to provide alternate accommodation for Cofis lead to the building of a vast number of council houses.

Richard Roberts recalls living in Pool Side as a child until the demolition of many of the houses in the street in 1963. These houses used to flood regularly with water from the culveted River (Afon) Cadnant – Richard once ran downstairs in the dark on his way to school to find himself chest deep in cold murky water! In order to stand today where this photographer was in the early 1960s you would have to be standing on the roundabout under the flyover. (Top photograph).

The men who built Ysgubor Goch

Ysgybor Goch; the inhabitants of Caer Saint host a Victory in
Japan party in September 1945

David Ellis

By the time the Second World War broke out, these sixty two men had
built 510 council houses at Ysgubor Goch on the rural eastern edge of the
town. The highlighted gentleman is John Williams, who later worked in
the butchers shop in Bridge Street and later still became the caretaker of Syr Hugh Owen School.
David Ellis recalls being told that he was the first baby to be born on Ysgubor Goch Estate. David was
born into an old community uprooted into a new place. A discussion thread on a forum on the local
BBC Website, which ran between 2007 to 2009, suggests the things that stick in people's minds about
this estate are the warmth of the people and the fact that despite having little, residents would share
what they had – a good place, they recalled, for taking your sponsorship form round from door to door
and for paperboys for getting the most generous Christmas tips in town. Clearly, even allowing for rose-
tinted glasses, the spirit of Caernarfon survived the move from the old houses to the new.

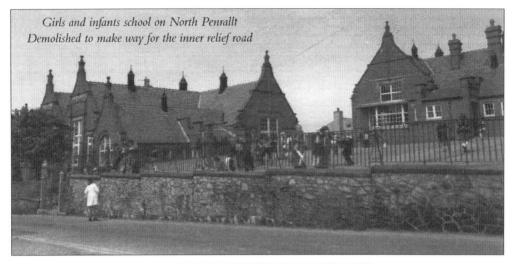

Girls and infants school on North Penrallt Demolished to make way for the inner relief road

This photograph of the children leaving Ysgol Rad for the last time is a part of changes in Caernarfon which included the demolition of houses which were not considered suitable for habitation and the building of large new estates on the rural eastern edge of the town. This Victorian National School was demolished, taking with it the memories of generations of children, but the new school was warm and the toilets were indoors – progress is not always a bad thing!

Segontium Secondary Modern School on Llanberis Road Closed in 2005 and demolished. Now the site of the new Crown Courts.

At one-time this was the headmaster's office at Segontium School How many readers stood outside this door waiting to find out their fate after some misdeed?

The Moriah Chapel, Caernarfon's largest Calvinistic Methodist place of worship

This long view of the Chapel was created as a result of the demolition of condemned housing stock over the road (Caxton Row) during the 1930s.

Built in 1800, the Moriah Chapel was destroyed by fire in 1976

The Cottage Hospital on Warfield Road, which closed in 1990

Houses are now built on this site and only the sign remaining to show where it used to be. For a long time Cottage Hospitals were funded solely by the local community – by fundraising, patronage by the wealthy and subscriptions and charges to patients. Later they often became incorporated into the NHS.

Galltysil Hospital, like the Cottage Hospital, the closure of this small hospital was planned as early as 1962 [11]

In the first decade of the twentieth century an annual performance was held in the Pavilion by the Caernarfon Amateur Operatic Society with the proceeds in aid of the Cottage Hospital. Later it would become part of Gwynedd Health Authority who closed it in 1990.

Galltysil was built in 1881 as an infectious diseases hospital for the Town Council by Mr John Hughes. Much good work was done here and one of our contributors to this book, Eurwyn Williams, recalls the wonderful work of the staff in saving his baby sister's life. During construction of the hospital workmen found the remains of a Roman Road in a good state of preservation. It was understood to be the road from the Roman fort at Conovium (Caerhun, nr Llanrwst) to Segontium (Caernarfon).

These two photographs clearly show the extent of the excavations and construction work needed to create the new roads. Siop Cae, the Twthill Hotel and the St David & St Helen's Church are clearly visible, left high and dry as though marooned on an island.

In Caernarfon the 1970s saw a major change when the town was effectively split in two by a new road, designed to bring relief to the town's increasing traffic flow problems. For the people who remember the change, the dislocation of the community is still keenly felt. It's not surprising when you look at the photographs taken during the road's construction – with piles of rubble as high as the lamp posts it must have seemed that the town was under siege. A considerable number of buildings were demolished including schools, chapels and hotels and the flow of the streets into and out of Caernarfon centre from the Twthill and Hendre areas of the town were cut through. Even the more exclusive Uxbridge Square found itself cheek by jowl with the new one way system looping around the Eagle Hotel.

The old railway station and sidings / goods yard site cleared ready for the building of
Safeway Supermarket in 1994

After the London and North Western Railway line south of Bangor was closed to passengers in 1964, the stations on that section of line became defunct and, like many of the others, the station at Caernarfon was eventually demolished. The track itself was completely removed by 1970 although the land around the station continued to be used for some years for a variety of uses. However, in 1994 it was all cleared to make way for a new supermarket. Initially this was the Safeway supermarket and in September 2005 it changed hands to become Morrison's. Times continued to change and in the 1990s another official decision was made; this time to pedestrianise areas of the Maes. This meant

New bus stops at Pool Side / Penllyn June 1994

moving the buses to Pool Side (Penllyn) where they are now. Ever mindful of capturing change in his home town, Eurwyn Williams carefully recorded this change on film in June 1994. Notice how light and bright this street was before the building of the multi-storey car park.

The first memorial or cenotaph to the dead of the Great War was a Celtic stone cross sited on the corner of the Maes and Tan y Bont (Greengate Street), unveiled on Saturday 27th September 1919

After the First World War Caernarfon followed the mood of the nation and erected a memorial to those who had been lost.

Four thousand people marched past the Cenotaph to honour the dead on this September day. The salute was taken by General Cyril Deverell Commander of the British 53rd (Welsh) Infantry Division, in the absence of the Prime Minister (also the local MP) David Lloyd George.

The *Caernarfon and Denbigh Herald* reported the event, explaining that the Prime Minister had been unable to attend owing to the strike of the railway men, which also prevented ex-servicemen from places like Pwllheli attending the ceremony. The paper stated:

"Shortly after noon the troops, assembled on Coedhelen field, fell in and afterwards, under the command of Major General Deverell CB marched through the crowded streets of the town, accompanied b the fife and drum and brass bands of the 2nd RWF [Royal Welch Fusiliers], the Lord Lieutenant (Mr JE Greaves) who was accompanied by Mrs Lloyd George, Major General Travers, CB, CMG, Colonel Dixon and Capt. Drage, taking the salute at Brunswick Buildings, Castle Square. The troops also saluted when passing the wreath–covered memorial to their fallen comrades, erected on the vacant space at the top of Greengate Street. The memorial, or cenotaph, took the form of a Celtic Cross, which was literally covered with wreaths sent from all parts of the county by relatives and friends of deceased soldiers, and by Red Cross Societies, and churches and chapels."

(Reported on Friday October 3 1919)

This monument was designed to be temporary however, with a War Memorial Committee being tasked with the job of providing the town with a permanent and more prominent memorial to the fallen in due course.

12 November 1922. Three years later this new war memorial was erected in a prominent position on the Maes and unveiled by the Mayor of Caernarfon, Councillor A.H. Richards. Sitting on top of this monolith structure, designed by Mr Rowland Lloyd Jones, county architect, the Welsh dragon watches over the square

Again we can look to the local paper, the *Caernarfon and Denbigh Herald*, to paint a picture of words of the event:

> "A guard of honour was furnished by the local company (A) of the 6th Battalion RWF and commanded by Capt. H. Gordon Carter MC. ... At 2.30 the solemn service began with the singing of the famous hymn 'O God our help in ages past', the band supplying the accompaniment". This was followed by readings from the scriptures, prayers and hymns. The Mayor addressed the crowd on the subject of the heroism of the soldiers and also apologised for Lloyd George's absence, this time due to influenza.
> "It was a moving and pathetic sight to see the widows and orphans proudly wearing the medals of their fallen husbands, fathers and brothers, reverently placing a token of remembrance at the foot of the memorial. ... During the service which lasted about an hour, the behaviour of the large crowd was all that could be desired. They came together to pay homage to the brave Carnarvon boys who had made the supreme sacrifice and memory tugged very hard at the heart strings of many of them. The beautiful wreaths they placed on the monument were the outward expression of their sorrow and affection. Even the children brought their posies and one little girl had written on the card attached to her bunch of flowers 'From Brownie to our big brave brothers'."
> (Reported on Friday November 17 1922)

Less than twenty years later Caernarfon was a town at war again, a second World War which after six years of hostilities would see further names added to the War Memorial. This ceremony took place on June 18th 1950.

Crowds of Cofis gather to 'Salute the Soldier' at the start of 1944s summer military fundraising scheme

At the point when the Allied forces were pressing their way into Europe, 'Salute the Soldier Week' was held to raise £100,000 towards replenishing the stocks of the army. A huge amount, but one which the Mayor had no doubt that Caernarfon would fulfil with a whole host of entertainments and activities. *The Caernarfon & Denbigh Herald's* reporter captured the spectacle in this article on June 23rd...

"A colourful array of flags and bunting overhanging the streets, draping the fronts of business premises and hanging from upper-storey windows, the glitter of the wind instruments of five bands, an impressive march past of a long procession representative of the Armed Forces and various organisations, and the town square filled to capacity by a huge crowd reminiscent of some of the great peace-time functions... Long before the parade started thousands of people had gathered in Castle Square, and the police were fully occupied in keeping open the avenues reserved for the procession. Some used their cars to get a grandstand view, while others looked on from upper-storey windows. The square was a sea of faces stretching down Castle Hill in the direction of the Quay... There were many children among the crowd; some of the girls wore red white and blue ribbons in their hair, while all proudly displayed their Union Jacks. It was obvious that many were watching a parade for the first time. One saw their faces glowing when, to the beating of drums and band music, the various contingents marched into position in the upper end of the Square. Prominent among the uniformed ranks was a large white golden-horned billy goat - the mascot of the Home Guard. It walked with the airs of one long-accustomed to parades. The contingents were headed by three Home Guard dispatch riders. On the balcony outside the Castle Hotel and behind the indicator and the stage, stood a Commando soldier, complete with camouflage and blackened face, and a Welsh Guardsman in his scarlet and black uniform." [12]

August 1945. This jolly looking Victory over Japan party in Pool Hill with paper hats and an accordion
includes at least three evacuees still living with their host families at the end of the Second World War.
(Boys 3 – 5 on the left hand side)

One obvious change was the influx of evacuees. George Naylor came here from Everton, Liverpool, not far from the docks which were heavily bombed. George and his sister were billeted in 'Caer Menai' with other evacuees. Initially they were schooled at a house in Church Street and later 'somewhere on the way to Twthill' – (Ysgol Rad?). Meanwhile local children were allowed to start school below the statutory age to release their mothers for war work – the tired little ones slept in the afternoon on camp beds. Once a week the evacuees were taken to the Guildhall to see a film – one that George particularly recalls is *Pinocchio* which came out in 1940. George was resident in Caernarfon until he was eight and remembers it happily – the trees, fields and beach were a world far away from the streets of Everton. Some evacuees were so entrenched in their new lives that they stayed in Caernarfon after the end of the War in Europe.

Another direct way that the war came to Caernarfon was with the establishment of the RAF base at Llandwrog in 1940 as a base for Hurricane fighter planes, stationed here on the North Wales coast to protect cities like Liverpool and Manchester from German bombers. RAF Llandwrog also became a centre of excellence for training of Bomber Command navigators, radio operators, bomb aimers and gunners. So it was appropriate then that on the east side of the town at Peblig Mill, Cofis working under Hunting Aviation were busily engaged in making important aircraft components including the manufacture and assembly of Lancaster Bomber fuselage noses including the gun turrets, hydraulics, bomb gear, auto pilot etc.

Of course war is full of tragedy and there are several sites of wartime plane crashes over North Wales. Roger Haigh-Jones recalls "My parents met during the war at RAF Llandwrog. My mother was a member of the WAAFs and my father was a Sergeant radio fitter (at one stage, I believe, he was involved in investigating why RAF aircraft kept crashing into the mountains nearby)".

Bill Watson (left) trained first at RAF Llandwrog.

Navigator Bill, Pilot Larry Carter and George Van Evry, Wireless Operator – Air Gunner, would later be tragically killed when their bomber ditched into Cardigan Bay during a night training exercise in 1944.

Residents of the newly built Maes Barcer (part of the pre-war Ysgybor Goch Estate) were happy to celebrate when the Victory in Europe was announced in May 1945

c. 1912 The local suffragettes make their point to the insurance
companies by setting fire to Caernarfon County School.
Joseph Hughes, the school caretaker, was not amused

War aside, Caernarfon was as prone to the winds of change as any town and as I write this book I notice that it's one hundred years this year since Caernarfon saw at first hand the fight for women's suffrage – the right to vote.

In 1910 the Committee Rooms of the Women's Freedom League (Suffragettes) were opened in Caernarfon High Street. On August 19th in that year the Caernarfon and Denbigh Herald reported that:

"Mrs. Pankhurst is announced to address a meeting in the town on Saturday under the auspices of the Women's Social and Political Union. The meeting, which will be for women only, will be presided over by Dr. Helena Jones. [Secretary of WSPU 1906]"

To promote their cause the Suffragettes held rallies and parades in the town. They even heckled Caernarfon's MP, and Chancellor of the Exchequer, David Lloyd George during his 1910 election campaign in Caernarfon, and later again during a speech in the 1912 Eisteddfod held in the town's Pavilion.

Eventually the Suffragettes' efforts became more radical and one method used was to do damage to public buildings – the intention here was not necessarily to harass the users, but to force the insurance companies to press the Government to take notice.

So, Caernarfon is a town shaped by world events, right from its very inception, and it may be that this has played a role in the town's strong character and spirit. Visitors will notice the survival of the Welsh language here as the mother tongue of the majority of its native inhabitants. Perhaps this reflects the determination of the local people to retain their own culture despite the imposition of other cultures over the top. After all, it was no time at all (historically speaking) until the Medieval strictly English Burgh of Caernarfon became home again to Welshmen and senior local government positions were held by Welsh gentry once more.

It was then quite a politically delicate decision to bring back the investiture of the Price of Wales to the town where it had first been held six hundred years before.

ROYAL TOWN

From the very outset King Edward I intended that Caernarfon should be a royal town and the castle was not only designed as a seat of government, the capital of North Wales, but also a royal residence. His son Edward II was born here deliberately in a strong symbolic gesture linking the castle to the English crown in 1284 and Edward I continued to emphasise this by investing his young son with the title Prince of Wales in 1301. However, he would probably have been disappointed to learn that he had not established a tradition, for it was not until the twentieth century that this ceremony was repeated here in Caernarfon Castle when the young Prince Edward, Duke of Windsor (later King Edward VIII) was invested with the title in 1911.

There had been some debate as to where the investiture should be held, but this letter which was published in the *Caernarfon & Denbigh Herald* on September 16th 1910 explains why Caernarfon was chosen:

"On Monday morning, the Lord Mayor of Cardiff (Alderman J. Chappell) received the following letter from his Majesty the King [George V] relative to the investiture of the Prince of Wales in Wales:
'Balmoral Castle, Sept. 5th. Sir, – In reply to your memorial to the King from the Lord Mayor, Aldermen, and citizens of the City of Cardiff, dated August 8th. last, with reference to the proposed investiture of the Prince of Wales, to which the above memorial so eloquently gives expression, I am commanded to inform you that in accordance with the wish of the Welsh people his Majesty has approved of this ceremony taking place in Carnarvon Castle during the month of July next. As to the selection of the place of investiture, his Majesty recognises that the city of Cardiff holds the foremost position in Wales as regards population, commercial importance, and the number of its national institutions; but in choosing Carnarvon his Majesty has been guided by the opinions of an influential and representative committee from the Principality. This committee advised that, owing to purely historical considerations, it would be more in accordance with tradition were the investiture of his Royal Highness to be held at Carnarvon Castle. The King greatly appreciates the loyal patriotic sentiments expressed in your memorial. I have the honour to be, sir, your obedient servant,

Arthur Bigge"

The Investiture of Prince Edward as Prince of Wales 1911

As you would expect there were great preparations made around the Castle and the town for this great national event. Even though a programme of works had been initiated forty or so years earlier, there was still much to do before the castle could be the focus of the eyes of royalty and the British Empire! Local landowner Sir Charles Assheton Smith even gave permission for two of his properties on the Maes to be demolished to allow a better view of Queen Eleanor's Gate balcony where the Prince would be formally presented to the crowds in the Maes after the ceremony.

Local men were employed to help with work on the Castle prior to the Investiture

On 13th July 1911 Prince Edward was brought to Caernarfon Castle to receive his formal investiture as Prince of Wales. Having been greeted by David Lloyd George in his ceremonial position as Constable of the Castle, the 17 year old Prince was led to the striped canopy where he knelt in front of his father King George V to receive his coronet as Prince of Wales. This coronet was designed for the event with daffodils and roses, and set with pearls and amethysts. Coached by David Lloyd George, who devised and stage-managed the event, the young prince was able to speak some words of Welsh.

The Prince, (bottom left of the picture), bare-headed in a simple dark tunic and white stockings, arrives at the canopy

The royal party then walked past the cheering crowds in the Castle and up to Queen Eleanor's Gate to present the Prince of Wales to the masses outside on the Maes and thronging the streets.

After the ceremony and dressed in his official robes and coronet, the Prince made his way down the steps, followed by King George V and Queen Mary.

The Investiture of Prince Charles as Prince of Wales 1969

Fifty eight years later another young Prince of Wales knelt in front of the monarch, Queen Elizabeth II, to formally receive his princely regalia. His coronet was again specially made, this time a more modern design but still using the traditional designs for British crowns; crosses alternated with fleur de lys. As for Edward's investiture, cheering crowds filled the streets around the castle. However, not everyone was happy – during the 1960s the nationalistic feeling in north Wales was demonstrated in acts of violence, and so security was ultra tight.

The striped canvas canopy of Prince Edward's investiture had been replaced by a Perspex canopy designed by Anthony Armstrong Jones and manufactured by a company based in Weybridge, Surrey. This allowed better light for the ceremony and for the filming of it too, not to mention to allow better viewing for the audience.

Erecting the canopy

A photographer was on hand to record the Castle ready and waiting to receive its eminent visitors

Prince Charles receives the official regalia associated with the Prince of Wales from his mother, Queen Elizabeth

Photographs taken by the Daily Post's photographer (not shown here) show the Prince doing 'walkabout' outside the castle, shaking hands with people in the crowds who had waited patiently for their view of the royals. Some had been in their place waiting for the ceremony for many hours and memories of the occasion are of the good humour and anticipatory excitement of the crowd. Not everyone in Caernarfon approved of the event and some people deliberately stayed away. But for those who did want to celebrate the investiture, street parties were held all over the region and a Prince of Wales Investiture Ball was held at Plas Glynllifon. A thousand people were invited to the Ball, and the Royal Family were represented there by Princess Margaret and her husband Lord Snowdon, whose own ancestral home was just down the road at Plas Dinas.

Outside the Castle Walls people from all over joined Cofis in the streets and the Maes to watch the public side of events of the day.

Street parties and celebrations

The twentieth century has seen a variety of Royal events – births, deaths and marriages. This series of photographs record Caernarfon celebrating these occasions.

Visit of King Edward VII and Queen Alexandra 1907

The King and Queen were in North Wales to lay the foundation stone for the new building at Bangor University. The *Caernarfon and Denbigh Herald* notes that: "His Majesty's knowledge of the way to set people at ease and his aptitude for doing the right thing at the right moment was evinced at every turn." And that the "visit has been in every way a brilliant success." (Friday 12 July 1907).

May 11 1910. The day after the funeral of the old King, Cofis wait on the Maes for news of the Proclamation of Prince George of Wales as King (later George V)

One of Caernarfon's Festival of Britain tea parties. Linda Joyce recalls, "my father Richie Jones is pictured on the first row second on the right. He says he can't remember which party it was, as he used to go round them all, leaving each one when the jelly ran out!!" [13]

The children of Henwalia enjoyed a street party in honour of the Coronation of Queen Elizabeth II in 1953. The Mayor and Mayoress, Mr. and Mrs. Richard Davies and Mr. Philip Davies the Town Clerk paid a visit to the party

These 1950s street parties would have benefited from the fact that rationing for canned and dried fruit, chocolate biscuits, treacle, syrup, jellies and mincemeat had ended in 1950, and the Coronation party may even have enjoyed extra sweets and sugar which had come off rationing just a few months before.

Prince of Wales Investiture Party 1969

David Owen Williams recollects: "This is a picture of one of the many street parties held during Prince Charles' Investiture in 1969. As I recall every schoolboy and girl was presented with a commemorative cup, which you can see many of the children are holding. I am the boy immediately in front of the pole, and the boy one third of the way from the left, second row, wearing a funny hat and serious expression, is my very good friend Elfed Jones."

Queen Elizabeth II Silver Jubilee Party 1977 – Cae Berllan

Martin Roberts recognises his mum with the long dark hair amongst the cheery crowd celebrating the Silver Jubilee in this photograph. She has her hand on the shoulder of Nellie (from the Corset Factory girls photo).

The children of Cae Berllan celebrate the Jubilee with paper hats and commemorative cups

Postscript

This is by no means the definitive photographic collection of Caernarfon's recent history. If I have missed out something that is dear to your heart then please accept my apologies. Nothing has been deliberately excluded, but the photographs that were available to me seemed to tell their own story and I hope that you have enjoyed it. When I first started the project which I called 'Spirit of Caernarfon 2010' I leafleted the town, asked people for their photographs and memories through the *Caernarfon and Denbigh Herald*, and talked to Cofis in the town and the world over, thanks to the instant communications of the internet. If I didn't come across you and your collection of old Caernarfon photographs then please let the publisher know – perhaps there is a second volume to be put together!

Two major contributors of photographs, Haydn Parry and Eurwyn Williams, both willingly trusted me with their collections. My sincere thanks must first go to them both. In addition, there are three websites run by Cofis which have been invaluable. They are David Williams's '*Caernarfon Memory Lane*', Keith Morris's '*Carnarvon Traders*' and Gareth Edwards, editor of '*Caernarfon Online*'.

So all that remains is to say thank you to all the people who have helped put the book together, especially Ryan Jones who has been enthusiastic, supportive and helpful right from the start. Diolch yn fawr Ryan!

Contributors:

Bill Barker, Ady Barlow, Jan Cooper, Caernarfon & Denbigh Herald, Gwilym Davies, Gareth Edwards (www.caernarfononline.co.uk), David Ellis, Gwerfyl Gregory, Martin Hearson, Sylvia James, Colin Jones, Dilys & Dafydd Jones, Eleanor Jones, Huw Jones, Reg Chambers Jones, Roger Haigh-Jones, Linda Joyce, Simon Millar, Keith Morris (www.carnarvontraders.com), Delyth Murphy, Doreen & George Naylor, Eric Owen, Gerwyn & Katherine Owen, Haydn Parry, Norman Phillips (photographs used in memory of Misses VA, KE & JE Roberts), Edward Povey, Raymond Pritchard, Hazel Roberts (nee Parry), Margaret Wyn Jones (nee Parry), Martin, Richard & Hazel Roberts, P. Simpson, Cel Thomas, Kevin White, Myra Williams David Williams (www.caernarfonmemorylane.co.uk), David Owen Williams, Eurwyn Williams

Other photographs reproduced with permission of:

National Museum of Science and Industry Library, London; National Library of Wales; Gwynedd Archives Service.

References

1   CADW, (2010) *Caernarfon Waterfront: Understanding Urban Character* p10
2   Jones, C www.caernarfonmemorylane.co.uk
3   Evans, K. 1972, *Survey of Caernarvon 1770 – 1840, Part II A*, Transactions of the Caernarfonshire Historical Society
4   Caernarvon Corporation (1909) *Caernarvon and its Environs* p28
5   www.caernarfonmemorylane.co.uk
6   Lloyd, L. (1994) *De Winton's of Caernarfon 1854-1892*, Caernarfon p31
7   Lloyd, L. op cit p34 note 52
8   Caernarvon Corporation, (c.1948) *Caernarvon, Its Industries*.
9   Hansard Commons Deb 21 March 1980 vol 981 cc900-4. Report by Dafydd Wigley
10 Caernarvon Corporation, (c.1948) *Caernarvon, Its Industries*
11 BMJ 3 Feb 1962
12 *Caernarfon and Denbigh Herald*, 23 June 1944 via Keith Morris, *Caernarfon Traders* website – my thanks to Keith for the use of this photo and his research into the 'Salute the Soldier Week' in Caernarfon.
13 www.caernarfonmemorylane.co.uk